The Sovereignty of the Accidental

The Sovereignty of the Accidental

Michael Brosnan

Harbor Mountain Press
White River Junction, Vermont

ISBN 978-0-9882755-6-0

Harbor Mountain Press is a non-profit press publishing books of high literary merit. For more information, or to donate to the press, please go to harbormountainpress.org

Harbor Mountain Press books are distributed by Small Press Distribution in Berkeley, California; for orders and more information about our titles, please go to spdbooks.org

Series Editor: Peter Money
Design: Andrew Miller-Brown
Cover Art: Molly Brosnan

Acknowledgments

My appreciation zigzags in all directions. First, I want to thank Peter Money, editorial director of Harbor Mountain Press, for finding one of my poems in the Irish journal *The Moth*, then tracking me down and encouraging this book.

Over the years, I've had two formal poetry groups—both of which have kept me in the game. A big thanks to Dory Adams, Catherine O'Neill Grace, and Steve Clem for our wonderful D.C. evenings of pizza and poetry. Thanks also to David Weber and Kendra Ford for both the wide-ranging conversations on poetry and the careful line readings.

Thanks also to longtime friends Rob DeBlois, Rich Horan, and Peter Dougherty. One's engagement in poetry has to start somewhere. Mine began with our youthful efforts at developing some kind of coherent worldview in the shadow of October Mountain, then spun out from there.

Thanks to my brother Robert E. Brosnan, Jr., for among other things, handing me as a teenager the *Rolling Stone* issues with Hunter Thompson's "Fear and Loathing in Las Vegas." Reading them, I thought, "Holy crap! We can write about anything!" And to my sister, Elizabeth Brown, for being such a good and generous and wise friend—and for always finding a way to the heart of the matter in every conversation.

Thanks, too, to my amazing children—Helen, Molly, and Sam. I'm constantly in awe of you. How is it that the three of you can be so intelligent and kind and have the souls of artists? Thanks also to Molly for the cover art, which so beautifully reflects the poetic world I tried to create here.

Finally, to my wife, Beth Brosnan. How many conversations have we had about writing, poetry, literature, film, art, culture, nature, and politics? How many miles have we run together? You make waking fun. You've also been my best reader and editor. This book wouldn't exist without you.

My heartfelt thanks to the following journals for publishing my poems:

"We Take Uncle John to a Party," *The Moth,* Winter 2016
"Aftermath," *Ibbetson Street,* Spring/Summer 2017
"The Year to Come," *The Cider Press Review,* January 2015
"Among the Volcanoes," *Confrontation,* Spring 2016
"Salt," *Into the Teeth of the Wind,* Volume XIII, 2015
"Saying Yes or No to One Thing or Another," *Muddy River Poetry Review,* Fall 2015
"Monhegan," *Puckerbrush Review,* Summer/Fall 2004
"Crow," *Prairie Schooner,* Spring 2004
"Acoustic Lessons," *Ibbetson Street,* Spring/Summer 2016
"Degas' Father Listening to Lorenzo Pagans," *Ibbetson Street,* Spring/Summer 2014
"Birds of Winter," *The Aurorean,* Fall 2017

P.S. The title of this collection is borrowed from Carolyn Forché's *The Angel of History,* section XIX—"The Notebook of Uprising." I deeply admire and appreciate her commitment to poetry as witness.

Contents

To my brother, Terence M. Brosnan

who knew well how to live and love

The Sovereignty of the Accidental

The Empty Lot, of Course,

Is not empty.

Is a tangle of grasses and wildflowers most can't name.

Is packed-down dirt and pavement fragments, battlefield bone-shards.

Is petted indifferently by wind-tumbling plastic bags.

Is Earth's first hint of astounding roundness.

Is the autobiography of where *was* went.

Is humming, maybe, sweetly like a daydreaming child.

Is another pure instance of synecdoche.

(One)

The Crazyheads

Agamemnon believed the imagined god Artemis
Demanded the death of his daughter, Iphigenia.
Big A was heartbroken, but relented.
So when he returned from the slaughtering war,
His wife, Clytemnestra, slaughtered him,
And their son, Orestes, slaughtered her
For slaughtering him, maybe with the help
Of sly sister Electra. Or maybe not.
All I want to suggest today is that you
Reread the first line of this poem.
Wherever you sit, look up, think about it.

The Start of Something

I was holding this thing in my hand
and I didn't know what to do with it.

It was like the word "'twould"—
familiar, yet strange.

In my hand, one might say, a can of stuff,
except no can, just the idea of one.

Pressurized, ready for release.
Waiting for fingers to intuit when.

At what moment does an exhale
carry more than its marginal weight?

Can answers walk from questions
with a dismissive wave of the hand?

When I was fifteen and living in the shambles
of suburbanville, in a town crowded with TVs,

not far from the sewaged sea,
I met a woman, a stranger, at the shore.

She was gathering shells and bits of plastic
and smelled like wild roses.

Her calves were smooth and strong
and her hands lightly veined, sure and storied.

I think she wanted to kiss me
as much as I wanted her to hold me,

but we just stood close for a time,
and stared at the objects in her hand

as she talked about how it all works—
the leaving behind of things. The loneliness.

Can you imagine me, years later,
on Fulton Street, in the hazy morning light,

spraying down the sidewalk with a hose,
washing away bits of fish and grime,

thinking about nothing in particular
and remembering this?

I was holding a thing in my hand.
I kept looking for a place to turn.

We Take Uncle John to a Party

where, with a small bird in hand,
he whispers

to a young woman
by the window,

"You know, if I had acted
upon my impulses..."

his voice trailing off,
going slack, along with his jaw,

because he can't recall
what should follow

after so many years
of holding back.

He puts the bird on the piano.
It shakes out its feathers.

I get him another drink
and we sit on the couch.

I love Uncle John,
but have no idea

what to say now.
And he doesn't want to speak.

Rowing, Winter

The killing cold sea
slaps gray against

the narrow hull,
keeps you coiling,

releasing,
coiling, releasing.

Life is big.
Today, you chose this.

But what have you chosen?
The rhythm?

The ever ache?
Over and over,

you dig
the cupped oars in,

feather them back,
dig in,

leveraging
liquid resistance.

Purpose? Halfway
across the harbor

in the bitter wind
and steady chop

you still cannot say.
Something about

truth clarified
in bodily limits,

in the racing heart
and muscle ache,

in loving the intricate art
of transience.

After the Hurricane

Anhingas, black wings
widespread, drip-dry

in Rhizaphora mangle,
like question marks

weighing the meaning
of the wind-shredded clouds

blustering by
and those blue brushstrokes

of sudden sky
slashing through.

But *wait wait wait…*
These are birds of the sea.

They carry sanctuary
wherever they go.

The gray, low-pressure fed,
deranging violence of this day

comes, gives way.
Wings fold, unfold.

That Book I Started to Read

There is it. Again.
A quick breath of thought
blanketing all that suffering.
There was a war. It's over. We move on.
The writer needing to push through
the ungluing pain, the hope-marring loss,
to get to a logical point.

I just stare at the pieces.
The "post."
The "-."
The "WWII."

I don't blame the writer.
He had to get to his point.
About life in America in the 1950s and '60s.
Interesting times: the cars, the music,
the rightful rising up against injustice,
the hollowing out of love. But still...

this thing we do, this reduce and package,
it catches me off guard some days.
I look out the window. It's late spring.

A gust of wind frees a cloud of pollen from the trees.
It bursts into the sky, dissipates.

The Insult Room

Let's set up an insult room, you said.
It was a joke. Then no joke.

You were reading *Moby Dick,*
and you read aloud to me:

"Hast lost any men?"
(Ahab to the captain of *The Bachelor* in mid-sea sail-by)

"Not enough to speak of—two islanders, that's all;—"
(captain of *The Bachelor* in breezy response)

The ships sail on. You stop reading. Look up.
Eyes screaming: Can you believe this shit?

We'll make it a work of public art, you said.
The world will learn how it feels, you said.

It will bear the whole heft of teary heartbreak, you said,
to show people what it's like

to live and work and try to love—*try* to know mercy—
in a sea of insults. Small ones, big ones,

ones that the insulter doesn't even know are insults.
We'll make it drip with intent, set it in a museum,

hire professional scowlers to menace every room,
you said. You said,

We'll install a wall of pulsing lights—brilliant and harsh.
Add head-throbbing sound waves.

Do you know someone at the Whitney?
Do you know anyone we can call?

Time Being Time

It's more an idea than a town.
But it's neither, though not nothing.

Time hates houses and borders
and walls and clean hair.

Through distain for bowls of fruit
it encourages the contemplation of art,

which, of course, it will also take away.
Though it's in no hurry here.

It loves rivers and snow melts.
The hazy after-spray of wind-smacked waves.

The way shoelaces break.
The making and unmaking of glaciers.

It loves the wobble of planets. Evolution.
Its own uneasy feelings about the emptiness of deep space.

It sort of likes history, but after a while
gets bored, walks away, and never looks back.

With great effort and expense we can bend time,
slightly, and to no known purpose.

With its feathered tail, time teases smugness.
The dirty banks of snow in late winter

are time's wry anniversary cards.
The slow death of loved ones—not so.

Time is its own drummer, no?
Forever's Ringo Starr.

Those dog-eared, clause-knotted,
slow-plotted novels of bygone manners

speak quietly of time's steady insistence.
So much language stilting into half gone now.

Time loves awakening submerged memories,
reminding us we're never immune

to moral catastrophe.
Then encourages us to forget.

Our clothes used to have so many buttons.
I think I might be grieving now.

Triptych, Unhinged

1.
Standing by the self-wounding peonies,
near a statue of Einstein, hardened in scruffiness,

you're reminded: The strange peregrinations
of the unconscious mind are not much different

from the strange peregrinations
of the conscious mind.

2.
The vaulted space in the stone cathedral,
when pushed to perform,

will hold musical notes beyond belief.
They just roil on

through the nave and clerestory and transepts,
lingering, as if asking you

to love whatever it is
that can't be unlocked from stone.

3.
You sit calmly at an outdoor table,
scooping out sections of grapefruit,

studying something written in quatrains.
Emanating from the bones of your hand

is the half-scent of self-knowledge
threaded through the rough draft of longing.

Why I Like Some Rocks Better than Others

Reading the newspaper while straddling
an erratic hunk of granite discarded
here in the New Hampshire forest
by the last passing glacier, I find

a review of a new car—some sleek,
hemi-throated thing that hugs corners,
hums along 16 miles per gallon, highway.
The ad speaks of muscle and torque,
leather and legroom.

After all these millennia—
gills to lungs, fins to feet, scales to skin,
unreadable eyes to handy expressions
for every subtle shift of emotion—
who would have guessed we'd evolve

into a creature that takes pleasure
in constructing something out of the Earth
so at odds with the Earth—desire it,
plunk down piles of money as if we thought
we could get somewhere this way?

The Hohokam built beautiful viaducts
and cliff dwellings. I admire them more.
But they are gone. Except for their art.

Apologia

For now, let's say the cliff
is a thousand miles away.
"Distant"

is a word
that comes to mind,
There are no stops, of course,

between here
and the there that is
still small in the heart.

Who laid the tracks this way?
No matter. After the invention of time,
it's just how things have played out.

Inside the train: cracked
cushioned seats, warmth,
a steady soporific rhythm.

A man in a bowtie
saunters down the aisle
touching the seat-backs for balance

on his way to pee.
He catches your eye, smiles,
keeps moving.

In his hand is a book,
a mystery, you guess,
because that's a good guess.

Imagine this, too:
there's an outside. Beyond
the world-muffling window

are tree-mad hills
and the occasional farm
where another kind of people

(tiny, it seems)
work, quietly tending
the fields with hand tools.

As you pass, birds fly up
from the trackside wires,
Now that you think of it,

more birds than you
would have thought possible.
You can't name them because

you can't see them clearly.
They are just birds.
Earth-toned. Winged. Reacting.

A river runs trackside,
bends and bends away
until visible no more.

The man in the bowtie
returns to his seat. There's something
about the way he walks.

A life subtly expressed.
It makes you feel you should
apologize to everyone for something.

But you don't know what.
You think you need to speak up,
but the words are hard to find.

Beauty? Grace?
...
The temporality all around?

Crow

One might prefer a fine salad with Myrtle Warbler,
but here we are.

You've plucked the blue-black feathers
and now with a serrated knife sheer

off beak and sharp slivers of crescent moon claws.
You've got the bird pinned with your left hand

and I can see you're afraid of crushing its skull.
The rice is steaming.

Remember how we met, my love,
and all the meals since over which we've faced only each other?

You can count the twenty most popular human emotions—
and we have eaten in their honor, just the two of us,

one of us talking and the other eating politely,
or together in silence

except for the occasional sound
of sucking on small bones.

We Talked

Ireland, I say.
Russia, he says.

Whiskey, I say.
Vodka, he says.

Joyce, I say.
Dostoyevsky, he says.

Potatoes, I say.
Borscht, he says.

I think about borscht.
He says nothing.

Out the taxi window:
America.

The Picnic Basket

I know I should speak directly. But directness eludes,
after the schooling—of being told by nuns

to read silently, then silently respond in perfect penmanship,
heartfelt, well measured, grammatically correct,

not to mention all those years of watching my own father
turn away from my mother without comment, walking

out the door to futz in his garden or take another walk
around the block as if there were something fresh to discover there.

So I'm writing to tell you... well, now I'm pausing
because what I want to say actually comes from another poet

writing about a painter who once said something
profound to a friend about the picnic basket of love.

Icarus Takes the Bus

It's a Wednesday night
and I'm waiting for a crosstown bus

and I'm tired enough
to imagine the worst.

Take, for instance,
the magazine on my lap

open to an article that argues
rather persuasively

that the Earth is deep in a dive
toward yet another mass extinction.

Three species per hour.
Thirty thousand a year.

I read it again,
slowly, mouthing the words:

Three species per hour.
Thirty thousand a year.

It's not just the loss of tropical forests
and the sieving of the sea,

but the heaven-eyed, carbon-fueled
longings of the peripatetic.

A big mess, this planet,
like a shattered lot

in the wake of a wrecking-ball death
of some forsaken dream,

where rats now scamper
in the random rivulets,

across the spill of words
like Devonian, like Permian.

Cautionary tales exhaust.
I know. And I'll be home

soon and I will settle in,
slip into a simpler mind.

Still, the wax that wings us
is thin and dripping—

Prolongation

I type "Blue Demonstration."
The computer translates this

to "Blue D most rational."
How cute, I think; this bold machine

that can't bleed wants
so badly to understand one who can.

Reminds me of me
last night, looking

out the open window
at the fox sauntering by,

wishing it would gaze in
with some hint of admiration.

Parenthetically

...(and yet Freud
said the Irish are the only people
impervious to psychoanalysis,
which, of course, makes me ask
if all our time together—the talking,
the emoting and overemoting,
the checklisting of dreams and needs
and the things we say we can settle for,
the brief admissions of happiness,
especially in the throes of sadness,
accusations of doublespeak, trickery,
deceptions tossed at one another
like ice-packed snowballs
with the desire to hurt, to *really* hurt,
the longing for that intense, wild-eyed
joy we both say we once had,
the frustrations with unapproachable fathers
and defeated mothers in love with unapproachable
fathers, and how, as children, we watched the world
without the slightest clue of what to think
of all the talk of God and damnation—
amounts to anything more than
a kind of perverse art form, the tallying
of irrational numbers, like reason rocked
in the loving arms of irony)...

In Shaky Town

I pull the map—stained, crinkled, torn, out-(no-doubt)-of-date—
from my pocket, study the gridded streets. It's too late
to determine how many lefts and rights I've made.

There is just forward with the which-way-now question.
And... well, as always, why?
No answer from the anorexic lemon tree, sky-
starved, whispering a haiku in this micro park:

> *Pathos marks this place,*
> *a swirling fog of frayed will,*
> *beguiling, but stark.*

God bless the lemon tree.
We should go left, I say to the pigeon
pecking a gravel-pocked cigarette butt.

Left is right with me, respond the soot-soaked eyes
of another Dr. T. J. Eckleburg overseeing
the slop of day with uncommon calm.

Until we hit desert or sea, adds the homeless girl,
shuffling in holey socks, waving brightly
at the lights refracting the always invincible rain

whirling in with the Pacific wind.
No advice from the broken trumpet in the dumpster.
Nothing from the forgotten and slain.

The sweat-glistening folks in the body-sculpting gym
strain against the drone of suggested indifference.
I love watching them through the window

as they grunt, steam, stink, chuff in place,
gorgeously determined. Do their bones know
the universe is still expanding—
a major exhale? Hear that, lemon tree?

That Look of Amazement

you give me some nights
it's the oblivion thing, isn't it,

a sitting-around-after thing—
say after a tough day

of work or failed play
and well into a second glass of wine

and not being able to say clearly
what happens to us all in the sweep of time—

you know,
eventually,

not having the words
not liking the words we have

about the meaning of love and
what came before the Big Bang

and why it did when it did
and how and how come

and who lit the so-to-speak fuse,
who needed to start so-to-speak time

and you say, logically, that the sun must die
you say this almost sweetly

and this planet will go cold
and dark like one of those

Dust Bowl homes abandoned
to the relentlessness,

and it all will just spin away

The Reason for Applause

1.
We like the ritual,
the simplest of routines,

the fulfillment that comes with fulfilling
the expected.

2.
Besides, it's too hard to stay still in the silence
after your heart's been prodded so.

It's our nature, even when it doesn't feel like our nature,
to give something back;

it feels petty not to.

3.
The sound of clapping is quite remarkable,
in-sync and out-of-sync at once, like hard rain—

a cleansing shower of unexplained appreciation
roaring out, but also washing back,

reminding us: we are here, too,
and we matter in this give and take.

4.
We clap to hear the clapping
as much as to hear the clapping recede—

the passing train, a summer wave
pulling back from the shore,

a sound that always reminds us:
there is someplace we must go now.

5.
Much of love is hidden in the folds of the hands,
difficult to extract.

The Year to Come

I get down on the floor, do pushups
until my arms shake and falter.
It's a good number, a number to build upon.

Kneeling, I turn on the television
to a football game in progress.
One team is winning, one is losing.

My wife has left me.
Fresh snow fell in the night
and I imagine my children on new sleds

being tugged uphill by another man,
their mittens drawing wobbly lines in the snow.
And out of this thin, shut-in winter air

small questions take shape.
Is it OK to drink champagne alone
and offer a silent toast to the coming year?

And how is it that shorebirds survive
in such icy water
with legs thinner than pencils?

Among the Volcanoes

At the end of the trail
in this land
of dormant volcanoes,
a waterfall spills
and pools before us,
clean, cold, subdued
among slick, glistening rock.
Beautiful, but odd.
From here, the water
does not run anywhere.
At least nowhere
we can see.
No stream leaves.
The water simply gathers
and reflects and remains
strangely still.
Of course, we're moved
by the mystery here.
We stand at the edge
and remark on it,
eventually bending
to feel its chill,
thinking about things
that seep away.

Church Light

Ah, Frederic, you always needed
to wave a dead branch

in light like this,
to remind us

that what we crave
is only momentary bliss.

(Two)

The Way Home

My pickup truck
sputters out of fuel

on a dirt road
high in the mountains.

What happens next
is a story of interest only

to those with the patience
for small movements,

those who can sit unhurried
on a hillside by the dirty

pockets of melting spring snow,
while all around

early wildflowers
spread their veined petals,

so papery, so implausible,
then close down again

with the fading sun
and the sharpening wind.

Salt

Of course the child wants to know why
I swim so far out into the morning sea.
Yet it's one of those questions

that catches me off guard, like the timidity
one feels talking about falling in love.
It wakes me to the world, I say vaguely, thinking

about the way one stroke feeds another,
the way miniscule bubbles rise off my hands
as I pull them through the water,

lifting them out into the lighter air and plunging
them back into the waves where the light
refracts wildly before giving up.

That, and the breathing, loud and frothy—
and how it feels afterward, standing on the shore
like this, towel wrapped, the heart settling down,

staring out over the fluid depths that buoyed me,
that gave up a sleeve of salt for me,
that didn't think to take me back.

Saying Yes or No to One Thing or Another

As long as the living live,
the dead will die and die again.
I'm reminded of this this morning
eating in a hotel in Portland, Oregon.

My mother died two years ago, and I...
I mourned her more than you'd care to know.
But over time, I could explain her life and death
to others in a few short lines.

She died at 84. Just slumped over one night.
She led a good life, and quit this sentient world
the way she had hoped: quick and with little fuss,
in her own home. God rest her soul.

Digging into my cereal, I hear her voice again
and see her face as it looked years ago, sitting
across the breakfast table from me, eating
out of a white porcelain bowl with pale blue trim,

telling me about the early years of marriage to my father.
She paused midstory to ask, *What's a grape nut, anyway?*
We laughed hard, too hard in truth, and then it was time
for me to pack my bag and head home to my own children.

We move on in life—not always out of choice,
and not always because it's in our nature to move,
but because we say yes or no to one thing or another,
and sooner or later we're miles away.

My mother died at 84. Just slumped over one night.
She was eating an early dinner alone in her beige
ranch house in the Portland hills. Her cane
resting over the back of her chair. On the table:

the *New York Times* open to a half-finished crossword puzzle,
her cordless phone, a plate with a chicken breast,
broccoli, a buttered slice of bread, and a glass of white wine
with a single, half-melted ice cube floating in it.

Birds of Winter

In the cold at the edge of the tidal marsh,
we stand among the dead, starched cattails

and check off the sea birds:

goldeneye,
goldeneye,
hooded merganser,
oldsquaw, grebe,
bufflehead,
least tern,
raft of common eiders.

Seen. Named. Beautiful. Wild. Inscrutable.

There's a wish, I think, for all this—
this hungering to know—
to settle into something worth shivering for.

Some truth
about the art of living and perishing
in the flow of things.

This feathering and uplift of bone.

But we grow hungry. The air grows colder.
We pull our coats tight and head for home,
the weak light fading fast.

From the marsh:

three geese rise in a wing-blaze,
race to find their V.

Veterans Day

From behind the photograph
of my father in uniform:

guns report.
Imagine my surprise.

Nickel-sized soldiers, little skittery things,
charge out and leap

over my splayed fingers, their tiny boots
clattering along the polished surface.

Again, I'm watching
the peculiar elastic webbing of life

stretch,
snap.

And to the memory of my father
who spent two staggering years

afloat in the Pacific—
his first boat trip—

puking, praying, begging
forgiveness from the mangled sky,

bluffing bravery and man-patting
the half-ghosted pilots as they boarded

those rattly Hellcats to be catapulted
over the South China Sea

into the wide open arms
of another twisted empire dream,

I say softly, and to no one, really,
"Holy shit."

Ponding

There's never nothing—that's the thing.

◆ ◆ ◆

Some days otters slink in and out of this tub of delight,
tracing and retracing the fluid shape of joy.

Some days it's the slow choreography
of unamused snapping turtles checking off
their grim-simple list.

◆ ◆ ◆

Some days one or more long-distance fliers—
green-winged teals, blue-winged teals, wood ducks,
common mergansers, Canada geese, mallards,
black ducks, pintails—careening north on tired wings,
or south on tired wings, in want of coolness, nourishment—drop

out of the sky, webbed feet splayed, skittering
into the wide wet welcome of the land's cupped hands.

◆ ◆ ◆

Some days the rain clamps down
and the wind sweeps the slate-gray surface clean,
except in the dark of early morning,
when what comes comes anyway,
so enamored with the delivering hour.

◆ ◆ ◆

In spring, after ice, sex-crazed frogs
sing their hearts out to lovers and predators alike.
Love me. Devour me.

◆ ◆ ◆

It's summer now,
the tail end of a slow-shifting August day.
Frogs conceal their intent among the reeds.
Damselflies, brilliant blue exclamation points,
prod the jealous sky

while the white-throated sparrows
weave their elemental wish into the pond's scrub edge,

punctuating the easy wind in the grasses and wildflowers—
the surround of sweet whisper.

I step in,

◆ ◆ ◆

hold my breath, slip
below the surface and feel a cold, buoyant joy
I can't quite name.

As always, the pond has my attention.
The fullness of it.
The stirring depth of it.

This isn't Biblical.
It's older than that.

◆ ◆ ◆

I surface and swim to the center
with long easy strokes, turn
and float on my back, feel the persistence

in the calm, steady current,
in the tannin-rich water welling up
from deep inside the earth and leaking
crookedly into the swamp's gorgeous murk,

while all around me, the trout—
these muscled shards of light — strike
quietly at the chaotic script of waterbugs,
whirligig beetles, backswimmers, boatmen.

◆ ◆ ◆

What better than to let the water chill me,
the current spin and keep me,
let the world speak through me—
saying what it needs to say,

while overhead, in their dizzying ballet,
tree swallows harvest every fleck of life
in the fading light.

Through Hell's Kitchen

Scientists now believe the universe is shaped
like a Möbius strip. Or perhaps a doughnut.
A finite thing, anyway, looping

back upon itself, seamlessly.
I'm walking along 53rd Street off 9th Avenue
on a bitter February night, heading west

among the gathered matter of past reason.
Blue-bagged garbage is piled high curbside.
Cars jammed in tight, dirty against dirtier banks of snow.

A faded dream of a bicycle choke-chained to a lamppost
lists like the final sigh at the end of the day. Across
the street: the beckoning neon hum of a neighborhood bar.

I know well that odor of damp wool and ache.
How time and worry tick on while the cook slowly stirs
the thickening soup of carrots, potatoes, basic hope.

And yes, there are people out here, too—but just a few,
scurrying, heads low, satchels tucked close,
faces cloaked against the herding wind.

I'm no Walt Whitman. I can't seem to celebrate this hour.
Still, I find myself observing everything
with a new curiosity, impervious to the cold.

My father lived here decades ago. Walked this street,
a young man half-prepared for the world.
And tonight I follow, a million paces back.

By then, his nose had been broken twice.
By then, he had lost his paltry savings at cards.
By then, he, too, would be out trolling

for the boost of simple wisdom,
accepting the quick and true smile on the face
of anyone passing through.

The Crossing

Waiting for the ferryboat, my son and I
sit at a table with a group of his friends,
eating pizza, drinking Coke, twisting napkins
into odd animal shapes. Briefly, I forget.

Then one of them points out a woman,
blue-haired, liver-spotted, wraith-lean.
Another laughs with a mouthful of soda.
It shoots out his nose along with the fractured notion
that we might age into something unexpected,
a parody of ourselves or a faint whisper
of what we had hoped to become.

I say, go easy...
but my voice trails off, knowing how it must be
for the young, who have little time for the art
of looking back while possibility beckons so.

What I want: to shush the room, turn to my son
and convince him to return home again,
keep things the way they have been for so long.
I want to say I can still carry him, if needed—

and I can—if needed. But the wind
fluttering all these dockside flags
speaks more plainly to the young: Come.

The boat arrives. And when he's gone
I peer up into the evening sky
and remember just how vast
this patterned, alluring universe is—
and how it must always hold something at bay.

Reading the Understory

Hunched in the tree-stand, gun in hand,
bullets in pocket, I whistle softly.

Out there: shagbark hickory, hepatica, starflower—
these are lovely, pliant things, too.

I fix the crosshairs on an indistinguishable patch of sky,
breathe in, breathe out, breathe in; hold it

and ask, What would *you* say
so much depends upon?

In the bleak light of a November afternoon,
a woodpecker, with its brushstroked crest of red,

arcs through the trees, gathers in its wings and slips
like a sharp knife through the wild knitting of understory.

Somewhere out there in the near distance, it perches,
slams loose bark, bug hunting. As one

with only the vaguest sense of how to belong,
I say, "Oh, my," then flick the blunt-nosed bullets

down into the mounting layers of dead leaves,
listening to them land with a soft ticking sound,

like the random falling of acorns
against the gathering ground.

Breathing Room

Cancer. Glioblastoma. Inoperable.
Will die. This summer. My brother.

18 years my roommate.
The one I know best.

Cell phones may be the cause,
or the crappy packaged food

we so adored in the shiny supermarket aisles
of the Long Island suburbs—

that luring landscape, safe, comforting,
and deadly in a million quiet ways:

the DDT sprayed in town parks,
neighborhood streets,

the wafting clouds of herbicides
greening the nearby golf course,

the small, dead, dyed pond
where we poked around after school,

the mercury leaking in the Sound
where we swam, where we

tossed horseshoe crab carcasses
at each other, laughing

and hoping to spear one another
with the sharp tail we took

for the barrel of an army tank,
as the sun toasted us pink, peeling

our pale, freckled, Irish skin.
Everywhere you look: a cause.

The myriad plastics, the methane
earth-burped from the town dump,

the lead in the paint, the lead
in the toys, the lead

in the gasoline fumes,
the preservatives, the food coloring,

the cigarette smoke, the arsenic,
the cleaning fluids, the sugar-drenched snacks.

And now, ladies and gentlemen,
he lies in a hospital bed

set up in his living room,
having traded in words for morphine,

riding out the final mile of a life that once
seemed endless and charmed.

It has all but stunned me to silence.
The speed of it. The haphazardness of it.

Bright memories
now flattened by a quickening finality.

A woman I know doesn't wince
when I tell this story.

My brother. Dying.
His three children paralyzed

by the loss to come, a wife bowed
against the empty sky.

The woman I know just stares at me
with a kind expression

and asks,
"What do you make of death?"

You'd think, after all these years,
I'd have an answer.

I shrug. "It's complicated," I start,
then stop.

The woman waits for me to continue.
We are sitting in a quiet room.

The soft sounds of the living day
float gently by the open window.

I draw in a slow, deep breath.
I love the feeling

of drawing in
a slow, deep breath.

I can't imagine it
otherwise.

Ode on My Factory-Second Grecian Urn

It's just an imitation urn from some shop's discount shelf,
but I like it nonetheless, its slightly out-of-shape shape,
its fragile, foreign feel, the way it freezes an imagined tale—
dramatic and ancient and undoubtedly false.
Behold the forever thin, one-eyed archers stretch
their bows and aim at a sky forever winged with dread.
Behold the lyre-limber women stuck now in mid-strum and pluck
as they sing longingly of unabashed love,
not exactly as it is, but as it is in mid-story, heightened
by the hurried weavings of chance and choice.

I could say I bought the urn because it connects me
to the ancient Greeks and their Grecian exuberance
for the shared life of everything sensual
and sexual and savage, or because, on occasion,
I actually think about Achilles, Agamemnon, Ajax,
those original alpha males, flawed but brave,
and how one might be a warrior in ordinary times,
or because the urn, even with all its easy failings, is art
and speaks about the nature of art, and frail beauty,
and the things we can't help but do to each other,
lovely and terrible—all at a price I can afford.

But, mostly, I bought it because I'm alone these nights,
in my basement flat, divorced and separated from my children
by a brutal document and a coastline of cities and suburbs
and the heart-stopping efficiency of a thousand fast-food joints
with their urine-spattered restrooms and their countertops

greased with the wafting fog of grilled meat and fries—
and so damn tired of letting storyless, unadorned glass
and mass-produced ceramics and recyclable plastic
hold my drinks, my flowers, my perishables.

Saw-Whet Owl

I have no particular place to go—
no errands to run, no friends to visit, no family to hurry home to.
I'm just driving through the dark—when I hear

the sickening thud against the windshield.
Backing up, I find a saw-whet owl lying in the road,
Warm. Limp. Mottled. Exquisite. Still.

I pick it up and place it on the passenger seat.
Dead, I'm sure, until it shudders, cocks its head,
staggers to its featherless feet, dazed, but coming around.

At times like this, what can you do but apologize
to all the little messengers of God skittering around our knotted lives?
I try my best to explain it:

the human restlessness, the carelessness accompanying introspection,
the *self* absorbed in its long drive for the unnamable,
confusing appetite with right, every day

the inability to see what we've truly done here.
Its ample, amber eyes, swirled with the truth of night,
try scanning what lies beyond the reflective window.

It rotates its head toward me, then away again.
No questions. Just a wordless wish for the obvious.
I turn off the radio, crank down the window and wait.

The owl bends its pencil-stub legs and fly-jumps
to the ledge of the door, hesitating only long enough
to confirm the world as it knows it,

which is not the world it should know,
nor the world we should know.
And when it flies off in a quick burst,

I stare at the dark space above the field
where the owl angled away, as if I believe
my eyes could ever fully adjust.

Long-Range Plan

Suddenly rudderless in a sea of my own making,
I hire a consultant to straighten things out.
He interviews me days on end—copious notes,
overhead projections of pie charts and such.

Every day, breaks at ten and three,
catered lunch at half past noon:
sandwiches some days, other days salads and bread
or Southwest chicken wraps, and always cookies and Coke.

We analyze my finances, discuss investment strategies,
identify the competition, delineate my strengths and weaknesses.
One Tuesday, he asks me to stand and announce to an empty room
what I do best, proudly, without the usual self-deprecation

one attaches to sentences about oneself in the company of others.
He tells me to remember that change blossoms from pain.
I was hoping more for "Be meek and everything's yours."
People I know are summoned to offer advice—

my parents, brothers and sister, people who say I'm a pleasure
to work with and those who feel I'm too distant or indistinguishable.
We graph it all, snap the pages into a three-ring binder,
stamp it "DRAFT." It looks swell: page after page

of my life as rising and falling lines, black and straight,
like a plotted course home from deep-sea fishing grounds.
Meanwhile, I begin to notice things about the consultant,
like the fact that he has soft hands and always smells of soap.

He has a fine watch and Western belt, too,
which he wears every day without fail. No wedding ring.
And he walks softly as if wishing never to disturb
anything in this world, especially strangers in the halls

of the companies he passes through for a few weeks
on end and then never again. I notice he drinks coffee
the first few days and switches to tea and stops eating
cookies altogether. And on the third straight day of rain,

after we print the second draft of my long-range plan,
I notice him touch his fingertips together and stare out
over the damp rooftops at the flags snapping in the gray sky
until he forgets himself and talks about the pets he loved most.

Years later, I'll explain it this way to my wife on the porch
of a quiet motel in Pennsylvania where we'll spend
the night after dropping our daughter off at college.
There are moments when you can't hold it together,

when the weight of it all pins you down, when the game
feels too much, and those you love seem almost strange.
Even the doe-eyed dog and those fabulous novels fail.
It's as if for a moment you've stopped the play

and pulled back the curtains and sat on the scuffed floorboards
among the ropes and wires and dented light fixtures
with the people you happen to be with,
and you take a deep breath, contemplate the oddity of life,

your existence, your fingers, your tongue, the weight of your calf,
your understanding of science and history and religion,
the remarkable chance that you are anything at all.
I'll tell her that the consultant and I sat close that afternoon.

For God knows how long we talked, then stopped and sat in silence
and watched the rain streak the windows with crazy crooked lines,
falling water that puddled below us, the new beginnings
of the little river that would float our little arks.

Mercy

At the crest of a hill
in the wind-scoured land
outside Lisdoonvarna—two nuns

sit quietly on raised stones
eating thin sandwiches, drinking tea,
habits flapping.

There are no trees here,
only the barest sprinkling of soil in crevices
of striated limestone where wildflowers dig in.

The nuns hunker and take small bites.
Mousy, I want to say, but not exactly.
It's something more deliberate,

as if peculiarly conscious of the act of eating
after years piled high with steady sublimation.
Meek, but fiercely so. I stop.

It was years ago
in a crazycrowded Catholic school
where I defied the nuns (not deliberately,

but just in the course of loving boyhood),
and took their threats and slaps
and afternoons of clapping chalked erasers

pretty much the same way I took snack time or math.
I have since learned of the strange and good ways
they've interpreted imagined whisperings of God

as they nurse the ill, as they deny their nature.
And now I want another look—at their faces,
at the texture of their skin, the movement

of their eyes, the boniness of their hands.
I watch them nibble away their sandwiches,
wipe their lips clean, hold down

the hems of their dresses in the wind.
Saying nothing. And when they stand,
it's their ankles I notice most,

thin and turned in above those weighty,
in-need-of-polish black shoes—never
quite attuned to this hard, uneven ground.

Monhegan

1.

There is all that ocean there
breaking steadily against craggy granite

and spreading beyond the lone lobster boat
to the haze-muted horizon.

And everywhere else
the sky is full of itself.

2.

All night, the ceaseless pounding of a half-flexed ocean
washes certain certainties seaward.

In the dark, silver-finned doubt sidles close
and cold, with its steady, silent eyes.

It's so long, this night, and black,
except for the stereoscopic spark

of stars
and phosphorescence.

3.

And in the morning by the shore,
a cormorant surfaces close to the breakers.

I watch its slick black body surface and dive,
surface and dive, eat one small fish, then another,

literally choking them down.
In time, it whistles away a wing's length

above the water, growing smaller,
a black pencil mark fading to thought.

4.
Tame deer graze in the field by the village,
as if this were the way of deer.

In the small, white clapboard church,
islanders sing—their gathered voices

pitched with the precision and care
of those so close to knowing.

As I board the ferry,
I strain my ears to hear

over the thrum of the idling boat
facing away.

5.
The island, in the distance:
a hump of granite

easily confused
with all that moves around it.

Tuesday at Nora Molloy's

Jimmy parks his van in the lot behind Nora Molloy's.
The bunch of us slip in the back door

and take the table beneath
the dusty moose-head everyone calls O'Malley,

though no one knows why anymore.
We order beer, all around,

and get down to the business
of shepherding out the last of our elders.

One by one, spaced apart in ways not to alarm,
they've all died: our parents, aunts, uncles.

Today it was Uncle Frank's turn.
The fireman. The last.

His daughter, Annie, wears his medal of bravery,
bright and weighty against the black sheen of mourning,

and tells us again how they'd once lowered him
by rope from the roof of the Gotham Hotel.

Sent to save a suicidal man, Uncle Frank thought *he* would die
as he spun helplessly in the wind, smacking

his bony shoulders against the city-stained bricks
fighting for balance and the one right word

that would give the desperate man hope.
She doesn't know what her father said.

It might have been a simple plea.
Or maybe he tried to joke the man down.

Or maybe he cursed the night softly
wishing to be home with his wife and daughter.

Still, the man jumped, sixteen stories
toward a scattering crowd.

Who's to say what's right in this world?
Who's to say that the neat rhythms of the Earth

won't go haywire and spin us toward winter,
never to return, or that the smooth alignment

of equator and sun won't suddenly wobble,
without mercy, murdering seasons?

Annie's eyes are a flood of love and sadness.
We all kiss her face, her cheeks, her forehead,

the tip of her nose, her lips,
which quiver then part wide in a thankful smile.

Tonight we've shut out strangers, focus on ourselves.
The drinks keep coming; simple food.

We're in no hurry to sort things.
From now on we are the ones

who will tell the stories—
with whatever omissions and flourishes we want.

This is our day—to reminisce,
to settle in, to find our voice.

It's Not Fish I'm After

I hiked furiously for three miles, heading
Through the cold rain toward the peak of North Tripyramid
It was fall, the leaves were falling, and acorns,
And the rocks were slick with rain.
Thoreau said something about a walk in the woods
Not being a walk in the woods if you think about
Life outside the woods the whole time, or even if you
Think about time—about getting to the peak and back
By, say, lunch. I thought I was being good.
I'd stare at the occasional tree and say Hello, tree,
Say I'm looking at you, little poplar.
I'd tell myself I'm not thinking about how messed up
The world has become, about the crazy election
And how it promises nothing but a world more frail.
I really thought I was doing well. I wasn't arguing
In my head with my ex-wife or thinking about applying
For a new job, knowing I'm losing my current one soon.
I wasn't worrying much about climate change
Or overpopulation. I'd look at the way the fallen yellow
Leaves rest on the rocks in the rain, admire the way
Tree roots rise out of the ground and turn back down
And seem not to mind us stepping all over them.
But the trail got too steep and wet and I wasn't
Even sure if I was on the trail anymore.
So after the third slip to my already aching knees
I turned around and started back down.
                                        And still I tried.
I began walking slower, breathing easier.

I looked again at said poplar and admired
How it just sits there taking it all in silently.
I almost didn't think about aging and death
Or how much I've messed up key moments in life.
I was close to being there, close to not thinking
About where I might get a decent cup of coffee
On the way home, and how damp I was going to feel,
Having once again forgotten to bring dry clothes.

Acoustic Lessons

How beautiful, I think, again,
standing in the guitar shop.

All these marvels of mahogany, rosewood,
spruce, sapele, maple, ebony, ash,

wild and sun-bound once, now kiln-dried,
planed, plied, curved, glued, clamped,

trussed, fretted, inlaid, lacquered,
tightly strung and precisely tuned

to feed our particular range of desire,
the varied rhythms and crooning blues of want

and regret and love and loneliness and exhilaration
and so on. I ask the clerk to take one down.

I sit on the worn stool, run my hand
up the back of the neck, admire

the complement of wood and wound steel,
press my fingers against the strings,

strum one soft chord, let it resonate, feed the air,
fade away. Then another.

Minor, major, augmented, diminished.
It was twenty years ago that I put it all aside,

fingers sore and tired, my sad-sack heart hammered
by the knowledge of what it would take to really know.

In my sorry head, Mississippi John Hurt sings,
voice half gone, but more sure than ever:

Cheer up, my brother, live in the sunshine.
We'll understand it all by and by.

Volition

The hornets build their paper nest
of saliva and bark above our back door.
Day by day, the mass grows, gray, ominous,

anchored to the eaves, while the hornets
gather from the garden, not the nectar sought by bees,
but any defenseless insect that pleases them.

The garden woos. The garden beguiles.
The garden whispers the need for give and take.
This use-and-be-used dance of volition.

We sit day-worn on the deck, the slow-to-fail
summer light so kind we've come
to accept this common carnage without flinching,

the hornets floating harmlessly over our heads,
except for that one time you tried to paint the eaves,
momentarily forgetting what happened in Eden.

Aftermath

This body, once boy-fired,
so bird-dog ready. Once unfettered,
indistinguishable from desire, pleased

to articulate the simple joy of ableness—
the sidearm pitching of flat skipping stones,
potato-sacking across summer fields,

spitting in mid-log leap, leaning
into the sweeping downhill turns
on my battered, ultramarine bike.

Even in school, I'd find the fulcrum of pleasure,
tilting the desk back to the self-balancing point,
pioneering new paths from pencil sharpener to seat,

demonstrating endless variations
on walking single-file
under a teacher's weary supervision.

And, after dismissal, romping along
to the amusing rhythms of gravity and friction,
among the young and their shared and private *yes*.

And feeding time. And the making of things.
And the loafing about. And the million gestures.
And the haiku of everyday body language.

And the eventual intimacy,
that initial shock of body-magic
one doesn't know one possesses until one tries.

Even if that were then, the lure
of locomotion still teases me out.
I can't forget. I still long to see what's there,

to run the engine down and ride
the afterglow of effort, that endorphined high
gifted to us through ten thousand years of the chase.

Today, what beckons is the cold Atlantic
churning in a nor'easter's aftermath.
I strip to my shorts and step in

and dive beneath a hard-curling wave
and surface on the other side and swim
beyond the breakers into that other kind of calm.

What I want is to feel the wild liquid rise and fall
of the sea, this elemental push-pull, to know
in the limbs again that sometimes perfect feeling

of wanting for nothing in motion, the heart
and mind and body believing they belong right here
in the slipstream of the possible.

(Three)

The Beautiful Indeterminate Something

Hammocked on black wire
firing

with disembodied
connectivity,

another deceit of blackbirds
glistening.

In the Primate House

Simian-slouching,
as one might on a Sunday night
toward the coming week,

you put one foot, then two,
in the primate house, the building
beyond elephants and the mock fox lair.

Here, flaccid gorillas huddle and grump;
gibbons and spider monkeys
chatter in a breeze of their own making.

Breathing deeply the smart smell of musk,
you whip back your hair and ape past the cages,
your lower lip thrust dumbly.

They are not moved, the others,
the way I am, when you turn suddenly
and orangutan-it toward me

and pause—your attentive face
mere millimeters from mine—and let your
quick, huffy, animal breath explain.

Your eyes, blue-gray and flecked
with green, and so dark
where the light of the world streams in,

narrow now, as your hands rise to my face,
touch my mouth, my nose, my cheeks,
slide up to grip my ears.

But you can't say it. It's so hard to say.
This surrender of raison d'être.
The quiet horror in wildness gone.

Quantum Entanglement

Warm summer evening.
Outdoor table. A café in Reims.

A bee. On the ground. Alive.
But in the calamity of premature death.

Half-buzz muttering. Resting.
Unable to rise back into the air.

Get the picture?
Here's what I know:

This bee, perfect in shape and purpose,
is for more than metaphor.

In France this year alone,
some 30,000 colonies. Dead. *Disparu.*

The culprit: us, with our pesticides, and manifest apathy,
especially, to this one bee—how essential

it is to the world. To all of us. To those who follow.
To how food becomes. To how we became.

The bee stops. Still.
I use my driver's license

to scoop it off the ground, place it
on a white napkin beside my cup of coffee.

I find myself wanting to give it a name.
I find myself wishing that art had more power.

That there were some arrangement of words
that would end this quiet storm now,

give both our species an even chance.
We are really quite beautiful, you know.

Cleaning Up

Exhibit A

My neighbor has synched a weightlifter's belt tight
to keep from blowing out his back as he bends
to kill weed after weed. He patrols in no particular pattern,
eyes down, shoulders slumped, searching for dandelions,
crabgrass, early shoots of wild violets,
and any of their broad-leaved compatriots
that love my yard and occasionally find a way
to hop the stonewall between us, aiming west.

His lawn: magazine green—a uniform,
domestic mini-savannah tended to please the eye
as he sits on the back deck in the evenings
and weekend afternoons, reading a newspaper or book
or drinking iced cocktails with his wife and friends,
loudly telling stories of youth and hinted-at wildness.

Although they laugh a lot in those hours,
there's no chance that any of them will live
to see the end of this new century.

Tsstt, tsstt, goes his mosquito zapper.

Exhibit B

What is difficult to comprehend
is that half the world's species, roughly speaking,
will exit with them, drained away
by these years of such uniquely human bliss—

this disconnected suburban dream.

My neighbor's name is Bob.
Boisterous. Generous, in his way.
Greets all of us with a smile and a handshake,
and the desire to say something funny about life,
confident about some blessing.

He once gave us a bag of bruised apples.

Exhibit C

Our biolinguistic diversity is disappearing rapidly, too.
By century's end, some 6,000 languages gone.

Not this one.
But it will be poorer for it.
For what it cannot subsume, harbor,
give new life to. For what it elides.

Sometimes I wake in the night
in a state of unguarded terror.
This is not exactly a non sequitur.

Exhibit D

Yard weeds.
Do you know their names?
Here's a short list:

Broadleaf plantain, Canada thistle,
Curly dock, Ground ivy, Henbit, Pigweed,
Purslane, White clover, Yarrow,
Mockstrawberry. Look

out your window. Look.
Name a weed.
A tree. A bird. There's something

about our blindness to the world as it is.
Something tragic in our stripped-down sense of home.

Exhibit E

The rabbit on the lawn: Northern cottontail.
It looks exactly like a sea mink. A tule shrew.
A Xerces blue butterfly.

The rabbit on the lawn is silent. Hears all.
Its ears are like twitching leaves of endive.
It sniffs. Haunches springloaded.

The rabbit on the lawn eats wild violets.
It loves the young bean shoots in the garden.
Sprints crookedly when the cat slinks close.

The rabbit on the lawn used to be a rabbit
on the lawn. Its spirit spies
from the shade of arbor vitae.

Exhibit F

What would this neighborhood look like
if we weren't so lawn-mad?

Houses set amid small clearings in the forest?
Clustered by the few open fields?
Resting high on the riverbank?

Each lawn is a brooch of prosperity.
It says we don't have to grow food.

It says we strut in the illusion of specialness.
It's the kind of thing that makes
summer evening strolls so pleasant.

Exhibit G

The mysterious *she* once said we write
to try to make something out of
not knowing enough.

Skill and recklessness is the poem.
Is the multivariate survival mechanism of weeds.

Exhibit H

This is the underside-of-Sunday part.
It must happen, some say: the Earth, self-correcting.

Others say it will be terribly sad.
Torturous, because it didn't have to be.

Cruelty is not blind to us.
My neighbor waves to me and grins knowingly.

We are on the same boat.
We are drifting down the same river.

I know why he grins.
I'm still puzzling over why I grin and wave back.

What They Couldn't Do

They couldn't tell the truth about you.
They hid some of the facts,
but mostly they didn't know the facts.

Didn't know you,
bound as they were by the tribal light
and rope of church.

That catechism—
it has so much right about living,
but often loses sight of love and mercy.
Fears its own shadow most days.

"Objective disorder"?

Blessed are the poor in spirit.

◆ ◆ ◆

At your funeral, a brother played a song of sorrow on his guitar.
The father did not stand to speak.

Were you in Purgatory? Hell?
The tears said he hurt. But he did not stand to speak.

The mother kept her face veiled,
returned to the days she held you to her breast.

In her mind: your eyes lock on, then that first smile.
It was perfect. It was God. It was love.

No one mentioned AIDS.

Blessed are those who truly mourn.

◆ ◆ ◆

1984. Seems so long ago now.
Had you known.

Had you been more shy.
Had you not needed love.

Had we not stepped back.
Had we not.

What you could have done—teacher.
What we could drink to tonight.

Blessed are the meek.

◆ ◆ ◆

A kind of blind euphoria:
The dogmatic "We believe...."

From the First Council of Nicaea,
the steady revision of the profession of faith.

The guessed-at love of the Holy Ghost
rivering on
among the quick and the dead.

The pain of getting it wrong
is not evenly shared.

de Tourquemada prayed for the 150 men
he allowed to be burned
"without the benefit of strangulation."

We're better. We're getting closer to *let love live.*
But the last mile will be rough.

Blessed are they who hunger and thirst for righteousness.

◆ ◆ ◆

Those last weeks were the longest.

We brought you things:
iced tea, sunglasses, magazines,
letters from friends who wouldn't come near,
clean socks for your swollen feet,
the last meal over and over.

I am not afraid of death, you insisted,
twice handing me a misspelled note of thanks
and farewell.

And when the priest bent
to absolve you of the sin of being,
your rage made me see.

Blessed are the merciful.

◆ ◆ ◆

Outside, in the shadows of trees
a young doe sampled the frozen,
bruised flesh of once-sweet apples.

We watched from the window.

Late fall.

Blessed are the pure of heart.

◆ ◆ ◆

In my bedroom, in the corner by the dresser:
An old, falling-to-pieces wicker hamper.

I rescued it from your apartment.
Use it to hold my dirty clothes.

Once a week, I heft it, hug it
to my body and carry it to the washer.

I think of you—thirty years gone and counting.
Once in a while, I duct-tape the edges to keep it together.

Blessed are the peacemakers.

◆ ◆ ◆

Sad that faith
can leave us

dumb.

Blessed are they who are persecuted for the sake of righteousness.

Self-ish

Not *selfish*—not steeped
in want and worry and wish.

But *self*-hyphen-*ish,* as in a sort of self—
the "self" knowing it is but a gathering

of cosmic dust and what have you,
holding steady for now but hinting always

at some deep desire to disperse, once again,
in the battering chop of infinity's wake,

remixing the what-was with the what-is,
rooting around always for the what-may-be.

Still, the self-absorbed self-ish self
can trick itself some days

into believing it is a near solid thing,
sequoia-like, deep-rooted and heaven-stretched,

or even part planetary—a hunk of rose quartz
or obsidian, somehow tied to the tectonic,

millennial-made, gorgeously souled beneath
the shifting smear of earth—shimmering

always with some oblique purpose.
The near self—

staring out a filthy window—
weighs this truth:

how the once passionate, now ghosted
rosary-decade dreams of a long line

of western Irish folk—potato diggers all,
back-bent by British brutality,

starved en masse, forced aboard death boats,
abandoning their land, love, language—

headed out across the reclaiming sea,
and pressed on and on and on until... well, me,

here in my meager room,
word hungry, a yard deep in February snow.

The self asks, "What do you make of this life?"
The self asks, "How did the story turn this way?"

The self asks, "Why do you always fall silent
at the sight of birds in the trees?"

And then falls silent
at the sight of birds in the trees—

those almost answers slipping back
into the slow-stirring mist of the mind.

Infinitesimal

What do you make of the woman
eating French fries late at night,
after her husband has gone to bed?

What do you make of the husband
lying awake in bed listening for clues to happiness?

◆ ◆ ◆

And what do you make of me thinking
in the second person this way,
shifting to third,
and asking the ceiling:

But who is she, anyway?
And where is love in the brain?
And why is love in the brain?

◆ ◆ ◆

And why is it that I long to have lived through a war—
any war—

where I would have kept a small, cryptic diary for my children
to decipher years later on a winter's night?

◆ ◆ ◆

I try whispering in the dark, "I love you beyond belief,"
and imagine her face as she opens the box and sees… what?

A striped cotton dress?
Some shiny elegant thing on a shiny elegant chain?

An official parchment announcing that a whale or a star
or a Vancouver Island marmot or an acre of Sumatran rainforest
or a placid-eyed manatee slow rolling in the mangrove swamps
off the Florida Keys has been preserved in her sweet name?

It's so hard to find the center,
five years after divorce and one year into a new marriage,
here in the dark, with a stick of moonlight
slashing across the floor

and then fading out
as the clouds roll in.

◆ ◆ ◆

I should be asleep,
my body twisted and limp,
my breath the unconscious
breath of the animal I am.

We should be asleep,
spooned and drooly and warm.

◆ ◆ ◆

A word I bumped into today is "ideogram."
Ideas as graphic symbols.
Examples: % or & or (the big head-scratcher) ∞.

What should be the ideogram for hope?
Or tongue-tied? Or that sneaky feeling
that you are an agnostic even as you pray?

Right down the street is "idioblast."
Strictly speaking "a specialized cell
that differs from the cells around it."
But this is not a word that walks easy on a leash.
It needs to run, to roam, to pee on distant shrubs.
It's dying to be taken out of context.

◆ ◆ ◆

It's comforting, somehow, to spend time among the I's.
To drift among all the gorgeous stuff within.

You can't help but laugh. You can't help but marvel
at how so many of the words combat each other

as if jockeying for attention, like puppies.

◆ ◆ ◆

Consider: ill-humored, illuminate, if

◆ ◆ ◆

imbecile, immaculate,
intone, intoxicate

◆ ◆ ◆

inquisitive, inquisition

◆ ◆ ◆

innuendo

◆ ◆ ◆

insatiable, insecure, insomnia,
intercourse, intrude, interlude

◆ ◆ ◆

itch, iron, irrational,
Ivan the Terrible, itsy-bitsy

◆ ◆ ◆

idyll, idol, idle

◆ ◆ ◆

You just want to gather these words up in a laundry sack,
pocket a few, like worry stones, to paw over on long walks
in the forest of self-forgiveness,

impale the rest on public fences.

◆ ◆ ◆

It's a Monday night. Lots of heavy, low clouds
heaving about the neighborhood now. Brutes.
But I'm not unhappy.
This is the state that puzzles me so often.
Being not unhappy.

◆ ◆ ◆

That, and the simmering need to know
what is juxtaposed.

Consider the two of us.
The moonlight and its penumbra.
Infinitesimal, infinity.

Landscape, with Moving Figure

Not hapless walking.
Not dog walking, even with dog.

Not a walking toward.

More an attempt

◆

to return to
some imagined point of

departure.

◆

A retracing
faintly tasting

of reassessment.

Plum versus pear.
What is it about choice?

◆

Birds chatter.
Your heart races.
Listen.
Don't grieve

◆

in this painting of yours.

◆

This—

◆

Do you hear?
Listen:

the cheery cheer-up-cheerily of robins
on fresh-cut lawns.

◆

Sleek cars murmur past.

A plane scratches out restlessness
across the suburban sky.

◆

So much to consider.

So much

◆

is reshaped

in the incessant whispering,

the wish
to keep stride with

the striving.

◆

In the mind's lush valley

velvet blossoms of choke-cherries
fall, letting go in the cool,

shadowy unraveling of yet another spring.

◆

The fragrance:

Easy Ache.

◆

What is it about choice?

The mind never tiring
of holding want and love to the light?

Don't

Don't be bored. Don't be trivial.

Don't be like that.

See how love and judgment can be braided. Braid them.
Swing them freely as you turn. Turn.

Be attentive. Even in sleep. Even after a third martini.
Even before the first.

Self propel.   Amaze.   Ignite.   Smolder.   Reignite.

Watch the fruit fly in the kitchen.
Such a short life.

Choose and choose and choose and choose.

Sear in *constant wonder.*
Those who have:
    The consciously spare
    Abstract Expressionists
    The idiosyncratic
    People you cannot pigeonhole

Ascend.   Love.   Something.   Fight.

Slow down enough to hear tone, feel structure.
  What you create *I know will be beautiful.*

I know I will love it as I love you.

Did you have a melancholy breakfast?
OK, then, you had a melancholy breakfast.

A wish half-prayed last night before fitful sleep:

> You need to live.
> Stay here.

When startled, most fruit flies choose light, but not all.

Evoke.   Smell like books.   Know the sea.

Degas' Father Listening to Lorenzo Pagans

In that simple room, bleaked with blacks and browns
and off-white light, Degas' dad sits, angled forward,
his forearms resting on his thighs, his hands folded loosely,
his face slack-jawed in easy concentration,

focusing now not on the room,
not on the guitarist playing to his right,
not on the others gathered around him,
but on the sound itself, the strummed chords,

the balletic arpeggios and sustained notes
that slip inside to the pit of his being,
and he can't help but cock his head, nod,
and feel a quaver of joy at the rightness of it all,

like the touch of Celestine's hand in the night,
or the ease of conversation with old friends,
or the unexplained resolve that comes over him
sometimes walking alone along the Seine under the stars—

and it *is* emotion he feels, the full, brilliant,
immeasurable power of it, and the remembrance
that emotions can be good, too, can transport us,
even after so many days of wearing us down,

after so many days of being the unwanted companion
in our waking hours, knotting our dreams, all is good
again, like the guitar, like the guitarist sitting upright,
confident in every movement of his supple fingers,

like the others in the room whom he now sees anew
and admires without the slightest hint of complication,
especially the son in the corner dedicating his time
to their time together, transforming this evening

for whoever might need it years from now,
for whoever might need to pause and feel
for those who also wanted to love this world deeply,
in a different time, which is the same time.

Ashcan School

#1

Ah, this smudged life,
lipstick-smeared

into storm horizon.
In the studio of spewing want,

walls striated with burnt sienna

and near-spoiled plum,
you've come

to complicate the hell out of the poor canvas.

Again.

#2

Every day and every

day,

the hurried kisses
in the dismal indoor light

cancel out near-kind gestures,

feed the veins of vulnerability limbering negative space.

What is shoved is shoved
with muscled longing
            into the shadow-

                    worn corners. Still,

at the center of things,
some "here" abides,

wanting to be pinned and released.

#3
A world of cold comments: hard conté lines
            checked upon the unfinished cityscape.

What purpose these piling-up slights?

Art?

How odd, you say and spit, stand back,
            roll up your sleeves.

#4
Last night, the scree of your dream sighs
gouged out the purer light of stars.

So now
            (dear?)

in the bird-whistling morning,
I can't help but stare proud, as your fingers

patiently trace
the painting's third-draft edginess,

feeling, not searching, for
the rim of authenticity in the

ever-mess

of asymmetry.

#5
You grip the Grumbacher's
ferrule crimp

tight,
like a carving knife,

present tense your neck,
squinch your face—

another mouthful of gin and vermouth.

It's time to tease the pigmentation
to tell

the harder truth.

(Four)

The River Is Everywhere

Out of the marsh, an immense
flock of starlings erupts

and careens wildly north, swept up
in its own invisible river of sky,

so many birds, night-speckled,
easily driven

by one small wing-beat,
then another.

And you, watching all this,
thought you had lost your way.

Dear Dead Days Beyond Recall

Did he ever hug you, your father?
I don't know. Possibly. Possibly not.
Or maybe not possible.

Try to focus, please.
I don't recall.
See the dog eyeing the chickens?
I don't know if the dog hopes to kill one
for pleasure or worries that she must protect us
from the steady terror of farm foul.

Don't deflect. Your father?
Yes. No. He wasn't mean.
Just seemed distant and tired.
Whatever he dreamt, he didn't say.

Why did you have an affair?
Wait. What about the rest of childhood?
There are lots of memories
I can vividly half invent.

We'll circle back. What about the affair?
Felt delonely—pressed.

That's it?
Couldn't help myself, perhaps.
Like the dog. Those chickens,
they taunt her daily.

Forget the dog and chickens for a moment.
Perhaps I'm a cad—you know,
since my father never hugged me.

But your father may have?
Yes, and I may have been lonely
and started looking for ways to feel less lonely
even if sleeping with another woman
eventually made me feel more lonely.

What do you miss about your childhood?
I can't recall what I miss most.

Really?
No. Not really. But it's weird
to miss what I can't recall.
Know what I mean?

No.
It's hard to explain.

But you do go back to your childhood often.
I know I shouldn't, but yes, I do.
At least I go back to a childhood.
Any time I want. I just open the window
and clamber through and I'm there.
It's quite remarkable. I can enter
my old bedroom and read a book
in that overstuffed swivel chair

my mother bought from the thrift shop.
I'm sitting cross-legged with a Pop-Tart in hand.
Crumbs are finding all the cracks.
The chair smells of cigarettes.
With my thumb, I rub Pop-Tart jam
into its cushioned arms.

So odor triggers memory?
I can walk into my second grade
classroom and smell the floor wax.
The room is full of short people—
boys with white shirts and brown ties,
girls in white blouses and plaid jumpers,
half of them with Band-Aided knees.
Such beautiful little ghosts,
food-stained, God-minded.

What's going on in there?
The nun asks me to play the bongo drums
I brought in for show-and-tell.
I'm not sure if I should play
with my fingers or hands.
She asks, and I try it both ways.
No matter. It doesn't sound good.
And I don't know what happens after that
because I'm looking at my hands in dismay.
At some point, the class is dismissed.

Did you really have bongo drums?
Yes. With those little indentations for the knees.

When were you happiest?
What kind of question is that?

One that people ask, even knowing its pitfalls.
Well then...
See the dog? See the way its body
is taut with anticipation?
It's a beautiful thing, even if pointless.

Should we take a break?
I was happiest when I didn't have to answer to anyone.
Or when running around. I loved my little body.

And now?
I still love my body,
even with its failings and flaws.
After all, it's all I have, and all
I will have, and it has taken me this far.
I especially appreciate the bones in my feet.
The weight they bear without complaint...

I mean, what makes you happiest now?
Besides the bones in my feet?

Yes.
Mostly, the improbability of stuff.
Take Cheez Whiz. Jujubes.
The Eisenhower highway system.
The head of the hammerhead shark.
The expanding emptiness of the universe.
The novels of David Mitchell.

When a carpenter I know associates rain
with a very tall woman he once loved.
It's beautiful, isn't it?

Let's get back to the dead days beyond recall.
If you spend the night atop a mountain
in New Hampshire in early fall,
when the nights are unnervingly cold,
but the stars are out in full, and the wind
is sheeting out of the northwest, washing
away the industrial pollutants, and you realize
again that we're improbable animals
on the only inhabitable planet for billions
of miles in any direction, or possibly forever,
and that we're spinning at 1,675 kilometers an hour,
and yet you are cozy warm inside your sleeping bag
and the person next to you has just kissed you good night
and turned away, and you're lying there knowing
that in a few minutes you'll enter something
called sleep—the daily practice-step toward death
so necessary for living—and that your sleep
will be peppered with a series of dreams
that will take you across time and reason,
woven with unexplained lust/love/fear, and that
in the morning when you wake, the sun—
our resolute, up-close star that fuels everything—
has painted the rims of the mountains
red and gold, and a fine, thin fog is sliding
through the valley below, enveloping
the north-stunted trees and ragged streams,
and some tiny bird impervious to cold

is singing lovely as it prepares
for the quick-to-come winter, and the person
who kissed you goodnight kisses
you good morning, well, then... well...
I'm sorry. I'm not sure why I'm trying to recall this now.

Something about your father and forgiveness, I think.
Yes, poor man. He worked so hard.
And I'm sorry for just about all of it.
But she was beautiful that morning,
and it's difficult to think beyond that.

Do you want to say something about the chickens now?
Mostly I admire the quick twitch of the neck
versus the graceful cautiousness of those stick legs
and those hairless, little dragon feet.
Each step so bewitching and comic
it makes me want to cry out for something.

Colloquy

The sea shifts
and the wind and the sand,
such polyrhythms—this earthly agitation—

among the billion stars and stray planets
stretching out multitudes of light years, plowing
into the on-and-on emptiness, searchlighting.

How such a restless mess could pause
long enough to hammer out the blueprint of a cell,
then multiply it, add flagella, flippers, fins,
gills, lungs, the whole gamut of sensoria, is beyond me.
But I admire the unfailing desire to crawl out.

Above the sea, blustered about,
gannets circle and rise and arc across the sky,
fold in their wings and plummet—
bright white darts piercing the slate-green
roiling waves. Such a gorgeous,

splattering response, this
syncopated wing-dip and rise
of body and heart,

this

inhale and exhale
of pure hungering after.

Michael Brosnan's poetry has appeared in numerous literary journals, including *Confrontation, Borderlands, Prairie Schooner, Barrow Street, New Letters, The Moth,* and *Rattle.* He is the author of *Against the Current,* a book on inner-city education that served as a basis for the documentary *Accelerating America.* He also edited *The Inclusive School,* a collection of essays on issues of equity and justice in education. For years, he was editor of *Independent School,* an award-winning quarterly magazine on precollegiate education. Now he serves as senior editor for Teaching While White (*www.teachingwhilewhite.org*) and writes often on issues in education. He lives in Exeter, New Hampshire, runs in all directions, and plays the Irish tenor banjo.